How to Analyze the Works of

THOMAS JEFFERSON

by Annie Qaiser

ABDO
Publishing Company

Essential Critiques

How to Analyze the Works of

THOMAS JEFFERSON

by Annie Qaiser

Content Consultant: Dr. Woody Holton, III
McCausland Professor of History, University of South Carolina

Credits

Published by ABDO Publishing Company, PO Box 398166, Minneapolis, MN 55439. Copyright © 2013 by Abdo Consulting Group, Inc. International copyrights reserved in all countries. No part of this book may be reproduced in any form without written permission from the publisher. The Essential Library™ is a trademark and logo of ABDO Publishing Company.

Printed in the United States of America,
North Mankato, Minnesota
112012
012013

 THIS BOOK CONTAINS AT LEAST 10% RECYCLED MATERIALS.

Editor: Susan E. Hamen
Series Designer: Marie Tupy

Cataloging-in-Publication Data
Qaiser, Annie.
 How to analyze the works of Thomas Jefferson / Annie Qaiser.
   p. cm. -- (Essential critiques)
Includes bibliographical references and index.
ISBN 978-1-61783-648-0
1. Jefferson, Thomas--1743-1826--Criticism and interpretation--Juvenile literature.
2. Presidents--United States--Juvenile literature. I. Title.
973.4--dc14

2012946166

Table of Contents

Introduction to Critiques

What Is Critical Theory?

What do you usually do when you read a book or essay or listen to a speech? You probably absorb the specific language style of the work. You also consider the point the speaker or writer is trying to convey. Yet these are only a few of many possible ways of understanding and appreciating a speech or piece of writing. What if you are interested in delving more deeply? You might want to learn more about the writer or speaker and how his or her personal background is reflected in the work. Or you might want to examine what the work says about society—how it depicts the roles of women and minorities, for example. If so, you have entered the realm of critical theory.

Critical theory helps you learn how art, literature, music, theater, film, politics, and other endeavors either support or challenge the way society behaves. Critical theory is the evaluation and interpretation of a work using different philosophies, or schools of thought. Critical theory can be used to understand all types of cultural works.

There are many different critical theories. Each theory asks you to look at the work from a different perspective. Some theories address social issues, while others focus on the writer's or speaker's life or the time period in which the work was created. For example, the critical theory that asks how an author's life affected the work is called biographical criticism. Other common schools of criticism include historical criticism, feminist criticism, psychological criticism, and New Criticism, which examines a work solely within the context of the work itself.

What Is the Purpose of Critical Theory?

Critical theory can open your mind to new ways of thinking. It can help you evaluate a piece of writing or a speech from a new perspective, directing your attention to issues and messages you may not otherwise recognize in a work. For example, applying feminist criticism to an essay may make you aware of female stereotypes perpetuated in the work. Applying a critical theory to a speech helps you learn about the person who gave it or the society that heard it. You can also explore how the work is perceived by current cultures.

How Do You Apply Critical Theory?

You conduct a critique when you use a critical theory to examine and question a work. The theory you choose is a lens through which you can view the work, or a springboard for asking questions about the work. Applying a critical theory helps you think critically about the work. You are free to question the work and make assertions about it. If you choose to examine an essay using biographical criticism, for example, you want to know how the writer's personal background or education inspired or shaped the work. You could explore why the writer was drawn to the subject. For instance, are there any parallels between points raised in the essay and details from the writer's life?

Forming a Thesis

Ask your question and find answers in the work or other related materials. Then you can create a thesis. The thesis is the key point in your critique. It is your argument about the work based on the tenets, or beliefs, of the theory you are using. For example, if you are using biographical criticism to ask how the writer's life inspired the work, your thesis could be worded as follows: Writer Teng Xiong, raised in refugee camps in Southeast Asia, drew upon her experiences to write the essay "No Home for Me."

> **How to Make a Thesis Statement**
>
> In a critique, a thesis statement typically appears at the end of the introductory paragraph. It is usually only one sentence long and states the author's main idea.

Providing Evidence

Once you have formed a thesis, you must provide evidence to support it. Evidence might take the form of examples and quotations from the work itself—such as excerpts from an essay. Articles about the essay or personal interviews with the writer might also support your ideas. You may wish to address what other critics have written about the work. Quotes from these individuals may help support your claim. If you find any quotes or examples that contradict your thesis, you will need to create an argument against them. For instance: Many critics have pointed to the essay "No Home for Me" as detailing only the powerless circumstances Xiong faced. However, in the paragraphs focused on her emigration to the United States, Xiong clearly depicts herself as someone who can shape her own future.

> **How to Support a Thesis Statement**
>
> A critique should include several arguments. Arguments support a thesis claim. An argument is one or two sentences long and is supported by evidence from the work being discussed.
>
> Organize the arguments into paragraphs. These paragraphs make up the body of the critique.

In This Book

In this book, you will read summaries of famous works by Thomas Jefferson, each followed by a critique. Each critique will use one theory and apply it to one work. Critical thinking sections will give you a chance to consider other theses and questions about the work. Did you agree with the author's application of the theory? What other questions are raised by the thesis and its arguments? You can also find out what other critics think about each work. Then, in the You Critique It section in the final pages of this book, you will have an opportunity to create your own critique.

Look for the Guides

Throughout the chapters that analyze the works, thesis statements have been highlighted. The box next to the thesis helps explain what questions are being raised about the work. Supporting arguments have been underlined. The boxes next to the arguments help explain how these points support the thesis. Look for these guides throughout each critique.

Before he made history by drafting the Declaration of Independence,
Thomas Jefferson began his career as a lawyer and plantation owner.

2

A Closer Look at Thomas Jefferson

Early Years

Thomas Jefferson was born on April 13, 1743, in the state of Virginia. He was one of eight children, two boys and six girls. His mother, Jane Randolph Jefferson, was the daughter of one of Virginia's most distinguished families.

Thomas's father, Peter Jefferson, was one of the earliest settlers in the region. He acquired 1,400 acres (570 ha) of land, creating a large tobacco plantation. He named the plantation Shadwell after the London parish where his wife, Jane, had been born. Thomas Jefferson and his siblings grew up on this farm, which the family ran with the help of approximately 60 slaves.

Thomas grew up roaming the wild Virginia woods with his siblings. From the age of nine he studied classical languages and literature. On August 17, 1757, Thomas's father died suddenly at the age of 50. Thomas was only 14 years old. As the eldest son, he inherited his father's massive estate when he turned 21.

College Connections

In 1760, Jefferson enrolled at the College of William and Mary, where he took a variety of courses. Jefferson was especially inspired by Professor William Small, who taught science and mathematics. The two formed a close professional relationship that would later help Jefferson make alliances with political figures and other well-connected individuals. Professor Small introduced his students to philosophy, rhetoric, and scientific thinking by holding regular lectures about philosophers such as John Locke and Socrates. Professor Small also included Jefferson in political and cultural discussions he held with other distinguished professionals. It was during one of these dinners Jefferson met George Wythe, Virginia's top legal scholar.

Under Wythe's tutelage, Jefferson was drawn to the legal profession. During Jefferson's time, there were no law schools. Young men who wanted to become lawyers studied under experienced lawyers. After finishing his degree at William and Mary in only two years, Jefferson studied law under Wythe. He was admitted to practice law in 1767. Jefferson proved himself to be an excellent lawyer, which led to his election to the House of Burgesses, Virginia's legislature, in 1769.

Monticello and Marriage

In 1768, Jefferson began construction on Monticello. The name, meaning "Little Mountain," was appropriate for the house Jefferson began building on top of a small mountain on the grounds of the Shadwell plantation. Jefferson drew up the designs for Monticello himself. He kept Monticello as his main residence throughout the remainder of his life, continually renovating and adapting it to suit his purposes and ideas.

On January 1, 1772, Jefferson married Martha Wayles Skelton, a young widow and the daughter of an influential Virginia landowner. Through this marriage, Jefferson would become one of the wealthiest landowners and slaveholders in all of Virginia, inheriting nearly 11,000 acres (4,450 ha) and 135 slaves when his father-in-law died in 1773. The two moved into Monticello while it was still under construction. Their marriage produced six children: Martha Jefferson Randolph (1772–1836), Jane Randolph (1774–1775), an unnamed son who died in infancy (1777), Mary Wayles (1778–1804), Lucy Elizabeth (1780–1781), and a second Lucy Elizabeth (1782–1784). Only Martha and Mary survived to adulthood. In 1782, Jefferson's wife died of complications resulting from the difficult birth of their last child. Although Jefferson never remarried, most historians believe he fathered at least one and possibly six more children with a slave woman named Sally Hemings.

Political Prominence

In 1775, Jefferson was selected as one of Virginia's delegates to the Second Continental Congress. The First and Second Continental Congresses were meetings held by a body of delegates from each of the colonies. They met to consider how the colonies could respond to escalating tension with Great Britain. The First Continental Congress sent a list of grievances to the crown. They set a date for a Second Continental

Congress to discuss how Britain responded to their complaints. It was from the Second Continental Congress that the Declaration of Independence and the Articles of Confederation, the first constitution of the United States, came forth. Although Jefferson was shy, he was a powerful writer of political ideas. He was elected to the committee of five in charge of drafting the Declaration of Independence in 1776 and chosen to write its main draft. Although the members of the Second Continental Congress would change approximately one-fifth of Jefferson's draft, he is inarguably the author of one of the most important documents in the history of the nation.

Jefferson was elected to serve in the Virginia General Assembly in 1776. As the Revolutionary War continued, Jefferson's focus shifted to establishing the values that would govern the colonies. He focused on three issues: outdated inheritance laws, separation of church and state, and education for all regardless of wealth. The most controversial of these issues was the separation of church and state. Although he wrote the Virginia Statute for Religious Freedom in 1777, during the Revolutionary War, it did not pass the Virginia General Assembly until January 16, 1786. Jefferson continued to support these foundations of liberty as he served as the governor of Virginia from 1779 to 1781. When he became president, Jefferson did not forget his commitment to freedom of religion, becoming the first president to host an interfaith religious dinner.

He entered public service again as delegate to the Continental Congress, now the governing body of the United States of America, in 1783. In 1784, he was sent to France to replace Benjamin Franklin as trade commissioner and minister. During his five years in France, he absorbed European culture, learning new scientific information and farming techniques.

When George Washington was elected as the nation's first president in 1789, he appointed Jefferson to the role of secretary of state. Jefferson served from 1790 to 1793. In the next presidential election in 1796, Jefferson ran as the candidate for the Democratic-Republican Party, which he and James Madison had formed. John Adams was the Federalist Party candidate. The Democratic-Republican Party valued America's connection with France and wanted to grant more power to state governments rather than the federal government.

The Federalists allied with Great Britain and favored a more powerful federal government. Adams was elected president by only three electoral votes, securing 71 votes to Jefferson's 68 votes. As the candidate with the second-highest number of votes, Jefferson became vice president.

Four years later, Jefferson defeated Adams to become the third president of the United States. He took office in 1801. In 1803, Jefferson approved the purchase of the Louisiana Territory from France, increasing the size of the United States substantially. He also encouraged Meriwether Lewis and William Clark to undertake their famous expedition to explore the new territory and the Pacific Northwest. The expedition began that same year and ended in 1806, leaving behind a legacy of scientific and geographic discovery.

The Louisiana Purchase was the pinnacle of Jefferson's presidency. Although he was elected to a second term by a large margin, the prosperity of the country floundered and Jefferson's policies began to fail. War between France and Great Britain led Jefferson to his greatest failure, the Embargo Act. It closed the country's ports to almost all imports and exports, which caused the economy to sink and did not have its intended influence on Great Britain and France. In addition, Jefferson still faced strong political opposition from a small but vocal faction of the Federalist Party that caused him to attempt to hamper their freedom of speech. In 1809, Jefferson's second term ended, and he happily followed the precedent set by Washington of stepping down after two terms.

Jefferson dedicated the final years of his life to the creation of the University of Virginia, which he founded in 1819 at the age of 76. He considered it to be one of the greatest public achievements of his life. Jefferson wanted to develop a new kind of academic institution where students learned to be leaders. He personally selected the location, organized the design of the buildings, planned the curriculum, and enlisted the faculty. The University of Virginia at Charlottesville officially opened its doors in 1825.

Later Years at Monticello

Jefferson spent the last 17 years of his life at Monticello. On July 4, 1826, exactly fifty years to the day after the Declaration of Independence was approved, Jefferson died. He was 83 years old.

Jefferson wanted to be remembered for what he considered to be his three greatest achievements in life—the three contributions to public service he felt had the most impact on people. Before his death, Jefferson wrote the inscription on his tombstone himself: "Here was buried Thomas Jefferson, author of the Declaration of American Independence, of the Statute of Virginia for Religious Freedom, and father of the University of Virginia."[1]

Monticello, designed by Jefferson himself, is a National Historic Landmark and a UNESCO World Heritage Site.

Essential Critiques

Benjamin Franklin, *left*, John Adams, *center*, and Jefferson helped the colonies become an independent nation.

An Overview of the Declaration of Independence

Historical Context

On June 11, 1776, the Continental Congress elected a committee to summarize the colonies' demands for independence from Great Britain. This committee consisted of Roger Sherman of Connecticut, John Adams of Massachusetts, Robert R. Livingston of New York, Benjamin Franklin of Pennsylvania, and Jefferson.

Jefferson was the natural choice to compile the Declaration of Independence. His first published document, "A Summary View of the Rights of British America," openly stated that Parliament had no right to govern the colonies. The text, published in 1774, solidified Jefferson's reputation as an accomplished writer. The committee selected Jefferson to be the primary writer of the Declaration of Independence. As Adams recollected decades later, although Jefferson was the second-youngest committee representative, he had "a reputation for literature, science, and a happy talent for composition."[1]

Although Adams listed other qualifications, the most important may have been that Jefferson was a Virginian. Adams knew Virginians prided themselves on being the first and largest colony. He felt the other colonies needed to defer to Virginia to keep their delegates content with the idea of the revolution. If they lost Virginia, the other colonies probably could not stand against Great Britain. The version of the Declaration approved by the Second Continental Congress on July 4, 1776, is divided into an introduction, a list of grievances against the British government, and a conclusion.

Introduction: Stating Personal Rights

Jefferson begins the Declaration of Independence explaining why it is necessary to break ties with Great Britain and become a separate nation. He writes that a "decent Respect to the Opinions of Mankind requires that they should declare the causes which impel them to

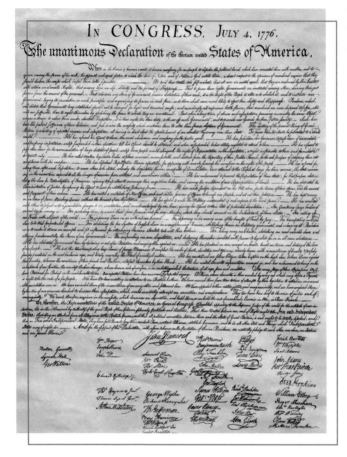

The Declaration of Independence, drafted by Thomas Jefferson, is one of the nation's most important and treasured documents.

the Separation."[2] This section borrows heavily from the political and philosophical ideas of the Enlightenment period.

The second section discusses basic human rights. It states that all men are created equal and that there are certain God-given rights governments should never violate. These rights include the right

to "Life, Liberty and the pursuit of Happiness."
The document states that governments exist to
protect these rights. When a government fails to
protect these rights, it becomes the duty of the
people to "alter or to abolish it, and to institute new
Government." This change of government should
not be for minor reasons. However, if "a long Train
of Abuses and Usurpations" by the government
makes rebellion necessary, then the people must
take action.[3] Jefferson charges that the king and
government of Great Britain are guilty of these
crimes against the colonies.

List of Grievances: King Exploits the Colonists

The third section is a list of the colonists'
grievances against the government of Great Britain.
Jefferson writes, "A Prince, whose Character is thus
marked by every act which may define a Tyrant, is
unfit to be the Ruler of a free People."[4]

According to the Declaration, the king of Great
Britain is guilty of 27 particular abuses. Each of
these abuses has been directed at the colonies for
the purpose of "the Establishment of an absolute
Tyranny over these States." Jefferson begins the
list by stating that the nation has endured the

king's exploitations patiently and that it is now the colonists' duty to expose the mistreatment to the rest of the "candid" world.[5]

The body of the Declaration of Independence is a summary of the grievances that the colonists have against the British king's abuses, caused by his interference and abuse of authority. For example, King George III disbanded many groups of colonial representatives, rejected many laws suggested by the colonies, and interfered with many laws regarding the colonists. He retained the military under his direct authority and maintained armies in the colonies during peaceful times. He allowed the military to have more power and authority than the colonial civil government and enforced higher taxes on the colonists to provide for the military. The king responded to colonial rebellion with brutality and hostility.

Jefferson writes, "In every stage of these Oppressions we have Petitioned for Redress in the most humble Terms: Our repeated petitions have been answered only by repeated Injury."[6] Since the British government will not listen to the colonies' requests for relief, he writes, the colonies have no choice but to take action.

Conclusion: Separation and Independence

The fourth section discusses the colonies' previous attempts to request justice and equality from their "British brethren." It reiterates the appeals for peace made to the citizens of the British Empire and how "they too have been deaf to the Voice of Justice and of Consanguinity [relationship by blood]." After many attempts to obtain justice, the colonists were left with no option but to "hold them, as we hold the rest of Mankind, Enemies in War, in Peace, Friends" and to declare independence from Great Britain.[7]

The fifth section formally renounces the allegiance of the original American colonies to Great Britain and proclaims the right of the colonies to be a free and independent nation called the United States of America. This declaration announces to all the nations of the world the 13 united colonies are liberated from British reign and all political ties with Great Britain are severed. The declaration also requests the nations of the world recognize the motivation behind this necessary partition.

The freed states assert the power to practice all the rights an independent nation should have,

including the right to launch war, build peace,
associate with foreign entities, organize imports
and exports, and govern the nation based on their
own laws and regulations. The citizens of each of
these new states have promised their lives, honor,
property, and commitment to the success of the
newly independent United States of America.

The document concludes with the signatures of
56 representatives from each of the new states. Each
signer endorses the document to show his state's
support of the Declaration.

Delegates from all 13 colonies signed the Declaration of Independence in the summer of 1776.

4

How to Apply Historical Criticism to the Declaration of Independence

What Is Historical Criticism?

Historical criticism examines the context of a document based on the social, political, and economic circumstances during which the document was originally produced. Historical criticism also analyzes how cultural and historical events happening when the work was written could have affected the final piece. The popular beliefs and intellectual thinking of an era heavily influence literary works. According to historical critics, awareness of the historical background of that time can shed new light on how to understand a literary work.

Historical critics ask questions about a work such as: What events were happening at the time the work was written? What social or political beliefs prevalent at the time might have affected the way the work was written? How might economic factors have influenced the work?

Applying Historical Criticism to the Declaration of Independence

When Jefferson was charged with composing the Declaration of Independence, the intellectual atmosphere of the country was changing drastically. People were being influenced by the ideals of the European Enlightenment, a cultural movement of the 1700s led by intellectuals and philosophers such as John Locke. Enlightenment thinkers questioned the necessity of a sovereign ruler. Now Americans were beginning to understand the importance of self-governance, practicing their rights, and using their own resources to benefit themselves. Although the primary intent of the Declaration was to declare the new nation's

Thesis Statement

The thesis states, "Although the primary intent of the Declaration was to declare the new nation's independence from Britain, it also conveys the pioneering views on independence and equality that were beginning to emerge in the American colonies." The American colonies were gaining new knowledge and ideas, leading them to question the need for a ruler who tried to suppress their growth. The new Americans wanted freedom of speech, freedom of religion, and freedom to live without external interference.

independence from Britain, it also conveys the pioneering views on independence and equality that were beginning to emerge in the American colonies.

Jefferson addresses natural human rights at the beginning of the document to set the foundation for his argument. In the Declaration, Jefferson uses Locke's theories to justify the demand for separation from Great Britain. Locke was an influential thinker and theorist of the Enlightenment era. Locke died in 1704, more than 70 years prior to the composition of the Declaration of Independence. However, his theories about personal identity and individual equality inspired the emerging radical thinkers in the colonies who desired democracy and independence from British rule. In fact, Jefferson regarded Locke's theories so highly he borrowed heavily from parts of *Two Treatises of Civil Government*, a document by Locke. Locke's concept of the natural rights of mankind is quoted nearly word for word in the Declaration of Independence.

> **Argument One**
>
> The first argument is: "Jefferson addresses natural human rights at the beginning of the document to set the foundation for his argument." The author will support this argument by explaining how Jefferson was influenced by the philosopher Locke, whose works addressed individual equality.

Without the use of Locke's philosophical reasoning, the Declaration would have seemed full of complaints. However, Locke's persuasive arguments regarding natural rights to life, liberty, and property struck an important chord in Jefferson's mind and in those of other Americans. Jefferson changed these human rights to include "Life, Liberty and the pursuit of Happiness."[1] Jefferson's Declaration simplified Locke's philosophies so all colonists, from aristocrats to common people, could better understand the issues at hand.

Jefferson challenges the old colonial way of thinking when he writes it is the civic duty of civilians to overthrow their government if they are being suppressed or tyrannized. Locke had challenged the theory behind the divine right of kings. This theory claims sovereign rulers had supreme power because God had given them their thrones. Instead, Locke believes civilians have the right to select their government and help create the laws

Argument Two

The author of the essay discusses an integral concept in the Declaration of Independence: a citizen's right to select a capable government that supports civilian development. The second argument states: "Jefferson challenges the old colonial way of thinking when he writes it is the civic duty of civilians to overthrow their government if they are being suppressed or tyrannized."

John Locke, an English philosopher and physician, was one of the most prominent Enlightenment thinkers. His influences are reflected in the Declaration of Independence.

they live by. In the Declaration, Jefferson writes, "When a long Train of Abuses and Usurpations, pursuing invariably the same Object, evinces a Design to reduce them under absolute Despotism, it is their Right, it is their Duty, to throw off such Government, and to provide new Guards for their future Security."[2]

These concepts were radical because, until this point in time, the colonial citizens believed the only way to coexist peacefully in a society was to follow the social hierarchy. This social hierarchy placed the king at the top of the government, and specific individuals were given power to carry out the king's commands. Historically, it had been understood that the government dictated the rights of citizens. As a result, it was the reasonable and lawful privilege of the government to have full control over those rights. Jefferson upset the established pact between civilians and their government when he wrote that an individual's rights are not set by the government. Rather, a government is dependent on its citizens for its power because it is the people who create and vote for governments. Governments may be overthrown or come to an end, but an individual's rights remain the same.

The ideas Jefferson proposes in the Declaration were radical enough that not everyone in the colonies accepted them as applying to all people. For example, the ideal of human equality is the main legacy of the Declaration of Independence. However, many colonial aristocrats—Jefferson among

Argument Three

The third argument provides a contrasting perspective. Radical Americans wanted freedom and equality for all; however, the elite colonists believed this concept did not apply to slaves. The third argument states: "The ideas Jefferson proposes in the Declaration were radical enough that not everyone in the colonies accepted them as applying to all people."

them—owned slaves. As they expanded the size of their plantations, their need for slavery expanded. Many also employed white indentured servants to work their land. The colonists were dependent on the nearly free labor provided by the slaves and servants. So it was no wonder these wealthy colonists did not consider slaves or servants to be entitled to equal rights.

Nonetheless, slaves and indentured white servants were coming together and rebelling against the wealthier classes. Bound by the similar issues of mistreatment and inhumane conduct, white servants and slaves were beginning to ask for rights and equal treatment. In this light, the ideas Jefferson expresses in the Declaration of Independence can be seen as dangerous and disruptive.

Implementing the philosophical and political theories of the Enlightenment thinkers, Jefferson wrote a document that openly challenged the social hierarchy and disturbed the balance between the elite and common people. The initial

Conclusion
This final paragraph is the conclusion of the critique. It sums up the author's arguments and restates the original thesis, which has now been argued and supported with evidence from the text. The conclusion also provides the reader with a new idea: these ideas, though radical at the time, became an integral part of US society.

concepts of the Declaration were unconventional and even radical for the time period during which they emerged. But today, these once-innovative views have become an integral part of the American way of life.

Thinking Critically about the Declaration of Independence

Now it is your turn to assess the critique. Consider these questions:

1. The thesis states that the Declaration of Independence encompasses new and pioneering ideas. Do you agree? Explain.

2. Do the arguments support the thesis? Are there any arguments that could be changed or left out? If you were to add an argument to this essay, what would it be?

3. The purpose of a conclusion is to summarize the essay. What does this conclusion say about the American way of life? Do you agree? Why or why not?

Other Approaches

A possible way to apply historical literary criticism to a critique of the Declaration of Independence is presented in the essay above. Historical criticism analyzes a document by considering the social, political, and economic circumstances that may have influenced the writer. Two alternate approaches for applying historical criticism to the Declaration of Independence are discussed below. The first approach addresses Jefferson's omission of women from the Declaration. The second approach considers the laws of nature and human rights, and how these rights were founded on both reason and religion.

The Founding Fathers

The establishment of the United States is usually credited to the Founding Fathers. The Declaration of Independence also emphasizes men, which reveals the strong patriarchal power during the early years of the country. The Declaration of Independence states: "We hold these Truths to be self-evident, that all Men are created equal. . . . That to secure these Rights, Governments are instituted among Men, deriving their just Powers from the Consent of the Governed."[3] Although "men" here could be seen as meaning "human," the truth is that women were seen as second-class citizens at the time of Jefferson's writing. A possible thesis statement addressing this issue might be written as: "That Jefferson did not mention the country's women in the Declaration of Independence is a general reflection of the times in which he lived."

The Laws of Nature

Jefferson draws upon various radical theories regarding the laws of nature and the rights of humans, the "separate and equal station to which the Laws of Nature and of Nature's God entitle them."[4] The foundation of these rights pairs reason and religion, appealing to two currents in colonial thinking. One invokes the ideas of the Enlightenment, which focused on human reason. The other invokes the authority of God and religion. By appealing to both God and human reason, Jefferson ensures his message will be heard and understood. A thesis directed at these issues might state, "Jefferson successfully appealed to a wider audience by incorporating the authorities of reason and religion into the Declaration of Independence."

Some of Jefferson's many interests included geography, mathematics, exploration, architecture, horticulture, and inventing.

5

An Overview of *Notes on the State of Virginia*

Historical Context

Jefferson's *Notes on the State of Virginia* promotes the natural resources and geography of Virginia. It also conveys his personal thoughts about the social and economic issues facing the United States of America. He began the work as a response to questions posed by a French diplomat. First printed in 1785, *Notes on the State of Virginia* was Jefferson's only full-length publication.

The book is divided into 23 chapters detailing various aspects and features of the state of Virginia. Jefferson calls these chapters "queries."

The Queries

The topics addressed in *Notes on the State of Virginia* are divided out by query but also grouped according to general topics. Queries 1–7 describe the state's physical characteristics. Jefferson begins by outlining the geography of the state of Virginia, using the rivers and tributaries to illuminate the longitude and latitude of the area. He discusses how to navigate the rivers, the best type of navigational equipment, and the distance between the bodies of water. He praises the majestic heights of the mountains and stunning views from the mountaintops. He also describes a variety of springs, waterfalls, and natural limestone caves. Then he moves on to the different minerals found in Virginia, such as gold, lead, copper, iron, black lead, gemstones, marble, limestone, clay, chalk, and salt, among others. He writes about the numerous types of native vegetables, roots, trees, and woods that grow in the region. He also writes about the anatomy and biology of various wild animals and livestock found in Virginia. Jefferson finishes his description of the state's physical characteristics by describing the extreme summer heat and frigid winter along with the rainfall in the spring and cooler fall temperatures.

Queries 8–12 describe the state's people. Jefferson begins by writing about the settlers that came to found the original colonies and the slaves that were brought over. He then outlines the enrollment of civilians into the military, their pay, and their accommodations in the state. He describes the "aborigines" (American Indians) who live in the area and the different tribes throughout the region.[1] He also maps out the numerous towns and counties that comprise the state of Virginia.

Queries 13–18 describe the state's laws and institutions. Jefferson writes about the British monarchy and the history of the state of Virginia. He describes local laws, the state's academic institutions, and Virginia's state wealth based on property value, roads, and buildings. Delving further into the state's laws, Jefferson outlines how the laws pertain to Tories, or those loyal to the king of Great Britain. He also describes the state's religious makeup and voices support for freedom of religion. He uses examples of times of great advancement that would not have been possible if not for religious freedom. He cites the founding of Christianity in Rome, the Reformation in Europe, and even Galileo's bold assertion that Earth is round as support for religious freedom. He also explains it is against all support of freedom to have slaves, and slavery does no good for the country. He asserts that no industrious people exist when they can make another person do their work for them. Jefferson finishes by saying slavery is so contrary to humankind's God-given freedom there is no way God will continue to give prosperity to America while it keeps slavery legal.

Queries 19–23 deal with the state's commercial and economic activities. Jefferson discusses commercial trade, import, and export within the colonies and Europe. He discusses fiscal properties, writing about the value of coins versus paper money and their depreciation. He also outlines the state's economic layout and fiscal responsibilities. He closes with the history of the making of the state of Virginia, describing various memorials, monuments, and legal papers that illuminate the state's progress.

Queries 14 and 18

Query 14, "Laws," is one of the most hotly debated passages in Jefferson's writings. In this section, Jefferson discusses laws pertaining to such matters as marriage, labor, farming, and slavery. But it is what this section reveals about his beliefs with respect to slavery and interracial relations that

is most under discussion. Jefferson states there are "real distinctions which nature has made" between whites and blacks.[2] He illustrates these with examples, describing both biological differences and psychological differences. These differences,

African-American slaves, deemed the property of their masters, worked on plantations with no pay and virtually no rights.

according to Jefferson, as well as the slaves' mistreatment at the hands of the slaveholders, "will divide us into parties, and produce convulsions which will probably never end but in the extermination of the one or the other race."[3] These two factors, according to Jefferson, will prevent the races from ever coexisting.

Query 18, "Manners," provides a contrast to Jefferson's statements in "Laws." "There must doubtless be an unhappy influence on the manners of our people produced by the existence of slavery among us," he states. Slavery provides "a perpetual exercise of the most boisterous passions, the most unremitting despotism on the one part, and degrading submissions on the other." According to Jefferson, people are imitative creatures. Children will eventually do what they see their parents doing. Jefferson challenges the people to provide an example to their children in order to stamp out this tendency that "transforms people into despots." Jefferson believes slavery robs people of their natural, God-given rights. However, Jefferson does see hope for the people of Virginia. He says, "The spirit of the master is abating, that of the slave rising from the dust." In the future, he sees the way to all slaves "preparing, under the auspices of heaven, for a total emancipation."[4] He hopes this will happen with the consent of the slave owners rather than with their destruction. At the time, this was a bold statement, though it is criticized by modern audiences in light of his other statements.

Although Jefferson argued against slavery, he had 200 of his own slaves working on his various plantations.

How to Apply Biographical Criticism to *Notes on the State of Virginia*

What Is Biographical Criticism?

Biographical criticism analyzes how an author's life affects and inspires his or her writings. Understanding an author's life facilitates a better understanding of the works the author produced. In other words, having insight into the author's life allows the reader to delve deeper into the author's intended meaning.

A biographical analysis of a literary work depends on grasping the perspective from which the work was composed. Biographical criticism does not focus on a biography of the author's life. Instead, the biographical information is used as a background to improve the reader's understanding, allowing the spotlight to remain on the original work.

Applying Biographical Criticism to *Notes on the State of Virginia*

Jefferson famously advocated for freedom and equal rights, but he fell short of granting these to black Americans. Although he held views that were liberal for his day, he was also under the influence of his social circle. Jefferson grew up in a wealthy, slaveholding family during a time when plantation owners and other wealthy colonists had great influence in the colonies. The upper class could not maintain its lifestyle without slaves and indentured servants. As a result, it is no wonder Jefferson shared his peers' views on the differences between the races. After all, it was Jefferson himself who wrote that humans are imitative creatures. Jefferson's contradictory statements on racial differences and equality in *Notes on the State of Virginia* reveal the influence of his upbringing in a slaveholding society.

In "Laws," Query 14 in *Notes on the State of Virginia*, Jefferson reinforces the widely accepted idea of the inferiority of blacks

Thesis Statement

The thesis states: "Jefferson's contradictory statements on racial differences and equality in *Notes on the State of Virginia* reveal the influence of his upbringing in a slaveholding society." Growing up in colonial America, Jefferson was influenced by slavery from the time he was born. He did not know any other way of life.

when he describes his views on the natural differences between blacks and whites. The color black and its negative symbolism were deeply ingrained in the colonists and their offspring. In *A People's History of the United States*, historian Howard Zinn writes that even before the slave trade began, the color black was considered "distasteful" by whites, both literally and symbolically. Prior to 1600, the Oxford English Dictionary defined the color black as: "Deeply stained with dirt; soiled, dirty, foul. Having dark or deadly purposes, malignant; pertaining to or involving death, deadly; baneful, disastrous, sinister."[1]

Jefferson also grew up with the social concept of black inferiority, knowing no other way of life. Long before Jefferson's birth, the slave codes passed by the Virginia Assembly had declared that Virginia's ruling class and all white men were superior to blacks. Jefferson explains the social stigma of the color black in his *Notes* in Query 14.

> **Argument One**
>
> The first argument supports the thesis, stating: "In 'Laws,' Query 14 in *Notes on the State of Virginia*, Jefferson reinforces the widely accepted concept of the inferiority of blacks when he describes his views on the natural differences between blacks and whites." The author will support this argument by analyzing Jefferson's views.

He writes:

> *Whether the black of the negro . . . proceeds*
> *from the colour of the blood, the colour*
> *of the bile, or from that of some other*
> *secretion, the difference is fixed in nature.*
> *And is this difference of no importance? Is it*
> *not the foundation of a greater or less share*
> *of beauty in the two races?*[2]

Not only does Jefferson question the physical beauty of black slaves but also their intelligence. He writes that they can be compared to whites in regard to their memory, but "in reason much inferior" and "in imagination they are dull, tasteless, and anomalous." Jefferson writes that he could not "find that a black had uttered a thought above the level of plain narration."[3] In short, Jefferson believes blacks to be inferior in both body and mind. He believes inherent differences between blacks and whites make equality between the races impossible. As per his views in the *Notes*, he was strictly against blacks and whites procreating children of mixed race because he believed this to be a crime against the laws of nature.

<u>In Query 14, Jefferson maintains and justifies the racial prejudices of the period by comparing slaves to land or property.</u> As early as 1682, Virginia declared all imported black servants were slaves for life. In 1705, Virginia passed a law declaring all slaves in the colony would be treated as real estate or property. Wealthy colonists and plantation owners grew up inheriting property and land from their families. Jefferson inherited slaves from his father, and when he married, he also inherited slaves from his wife's family. In any given year, Jefferson was reported to have owned 200 slaves, spread out through his various estates and plantations.

In Query 14, Jefferson writes, "Slaves pass by descent and dower as lands do." He also writes that along with lands and property, slaves are "entailable."[4] The word *entail* means "to fix a person in a particular condition."[5] The Virginia law of 1682 ensured slaves were entailable and remained slaves for life. One driving force behind

Argument Two

The author provides a second argument: "In Query 14, Jefferson maintains and justifies the racial prejudices of the period by comparing slaves to land or property." The author will support this argument by discussing the laws of the time, which held that slaves were the property of their owners.

this law was that slaves were an integral part of colonial life. Jefferson himself grew up on a large estate where slaves were essential to running a successful plantation and vast household. Like any other tools used on the plantation, the slaves were his family's property. They could be bought or sold like anything else on the plantation. Selling slaves to raise money was a common practice in colonial America. Slave owners used the law to their advantage and treated slaves as the law allowed, as real estate or property. After his death, Jefferson's property—which included his slaves—was sold to pay off his debts.

However, in "Manners," Query 18 in *Notes on the State of Virginia*, Jefferson deviates from the views of his time to propose his own vision for the future of slavery. Jefferson writes that personal behavior is shaped by social pressures, believing the young white children who see the mistreatment of slaves will likewise mistreat their own slaves as adults. The child puts on the

Argument Three
The author provides a contrasting example with the final argument: "However, in 'Manners,' Query 18 in *Notes on the State of Virginia*, Jefferson deviates from the views of his time to propose his own vision for the future of slavery." The author will examine Jefferson's viewpoint on human psychology in this argument.

"same airs" and is "nursed, educated, and daily exercised in tyranny."[6] Similar to these children, Jefferson was taught the dynamic between master and slave throughout his childhood. However, Jefferson sees this as problematic in view of his own beliefs about natural rights. Jefferson seems at times to believe slavery goes against the idea of natural rights. In his section on "Manners," he asks, "And can the liberties of a nation be thought secure when we have removed their only firm basis, a conviction in the minds of the people that these liberties are of the gift of God?"[7] This quote shows Jefferson recognizes a contradiction between slavery and the words he wrote in the Declaration of Independence: "We hold these Truths to be self-evident, that all Men are created equal, that they are endowed by their Creator with certain unalienable Rights, that among these are Life, Liberty and the pursuit of Happiness."[8] If men are given the right of liberty by God, how can the government keep that freedom from slaves? He then calls on the people to stamp out this practice that "transforms [people] into despots."[9] In the end, he predicts slaves are headed, "under the auspices of heaven, for a total emancipation."[10] Still, despite this proposal, many

Conclusion

This final paragraph is the conclusion of the critique. It sums up the author's arguments and partially restates the original thesis, which has now been argued and supported with evidence from the text. The conclusion also provides the reader with a new idea: that *Notes on the State of Virginia* follows most of the prejudices of the time, but also provides a platform for Jefferson to argue for the end of slavery.

of his attitudes toward blacks still show the prejudices with which he was raised.

Jefferson's aristocratic upbringing on a large estate with servants and slaves cemented his beliefs regarding racial minorities and slavery. In many ways, *Notes on the State of Virginia* fits with the laws and thoughts of the time, reinforcing the widely accepted concept of racial inferiority and natural differences between blacks and whites. However, despite his own prejudices, Jefferson proposes a future without slavery, following his philosophy of the natural rights of all men.

Thinking Critically about *Notes on the State of Virginia*

Now it is your turn to assess the critique. Consider these questions:

1. The thesis statement stresses that Jefferson's upbringing on a large plantation with slaves influenced his entire life. Do you agree? Explain.

2. The essay states that the color black, and by extension black people, had negative associations during this era. Black was considered inferior and malevolent, while white was superior and pure. Based on what you read in the essay, was Jefferson influenced by this belief system? Explain.

3. The conclusion should restate the thesis and the main arguments of the essay. Does this conclusion do so effectively? Why or why not?

Other Approaches

A possible way to apply biographical criticism to a critique of *Notes on the State of Virginia* is highlighted in the essay above. Biographical criticism analyzes how an author's literary works are inspired by his or her life. Knowing an author's background allows the reader to delve deep into the author's meaning. Two alternate approaches for applying biographical criticism to *Notes on the State of Virginia* are discussed below. The first approach analyzes Jefferson's belief that the black color of slaves' skin prohibits their freedom. The second approach considers how Jefferson's exposure to slavery from a young age shaped his ideas about race.

The Color Black

In *Notes on the State of Virginia,* Jefferson reinforces the idea that race is the significant difference between slaves and their masters in America. He implies that the fact that slaves are black is their main barrier to obtaining freedom, saying, "This unfortunate difference of colour, and perhaps of faculty, is a powerful obstacle to the emancipation of these people."[11] A possible biographical criticism addressing this contradiction might state, "Thomas Jefferson allows his reason to be affected by his society's standards of beauty when he condemns African Americans as inferior because their skin is black, a color his society believed was ugly."

Starting Young

Jefferson believes humans are imitative creatures and they learn by what they observe in their social environment. His own beliefs about the differences between the races were founded in his own experiences growing up in a slaveholding family. However, during the period of the American Revolution, Jefferson reexamined his beliefs about individual rights and freedoms. A thesis for a critique addressing this change could state, "Jefferson's experiences as a pivotal character in the American Revolution changed his early ideas about individual rights and freedoms with respect to slaves."

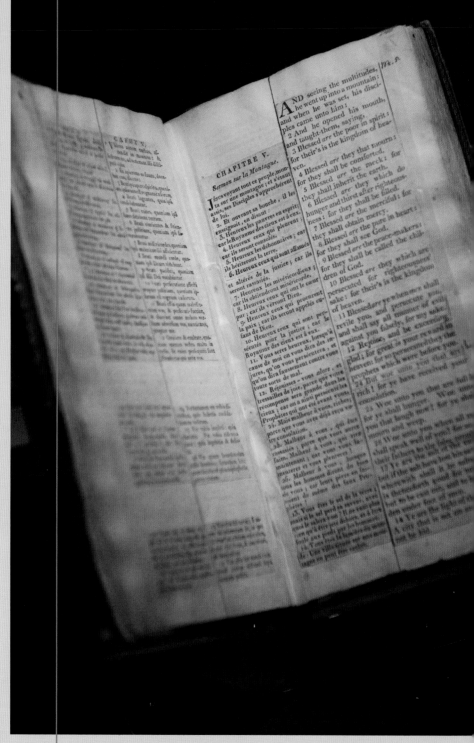

The Jefferson Bible is a testament to how the Enlightenment affected Jefferson's religious beliefs.

An Overview of *The Life and Morals of Jesus of Nazareth*

Historical Context

The Life and Morals of Jesus of Nazareth, also known as the Jefferson Bible, is a religious text Jefferson compiled in 1820. He did not rewrite the Bible but rather created an edited version of the New Testament by cutting and pasting excerpts into a blank book. The excerpts he retained best exemplify his beliefs about religion. He aimed to focus on the concrete teachings of Jesus by omitting passages that described mystical and unexplained phenomena, such as miracles performed by Jesus.

In a personal letter to John Adams dated October 12, 1813, Jefferson attempts to explain his reasoning behind compiling such a text. "We must reduce our volume to the simple Evangelists, select, even from them, the very words only of Jesus," he writes. They must avoid the words of those who are "giving their own misconceptions as his dicta, and expressing unintelligibly for others what they had not understood themselves." Jefferson states that he has already undertaken this activity himself, "by cutting verse by verse out of the printed book."[1] Though the Jefferson Bible was originally intended for his personal use, the text was published in 1904.

Jefferson's Selections

Jefferson was a deist. Deists believe there are no religious miracles and that Christianity's holy scriptures were written by men rather than being divinely inspired truths. Accordingly, Jefferson's version of the Bible focuses on the moral teachings of Jesus. To accomplish this, Jefferson deletes parts of the scriptures he cannot explain scientifically. All allusions to the divinity of Jesus are eliminated. No unexplained miracles are included. In fact, when a moral principle is mentioned in a mystical setting, the moral teaching is extracted, the miracle is removed, and the context is changed to focus on the principle.

One example of Jefferson's emphasis on the moral teachings of the Gospels is found in Chapter 3 of the Jefferson Bible. Chapter 3 contains nearly all of the Sermon on the Mount, found in chapters 5–7 of the book of Matthew in a traditional Bible. It begins with the famous Beatitudes and lists how a moral person should live. Because of its emphasis on morality, the Sermon on the Mount is kept almost entirely intact. The only part removed is when Jesus mentions prophesying and casting out demons. Jefferson also skips all of Matthew 8, which details several miracles performed by Jesus.

Perhaps the most striking omission Jefferson makes is that of the resurrection of Jesus. In the Jefferson Bible 17:29–52, Jefferson includes most of the details of the crucifixion from the four Gospels. However, Jefferson skips over Matthew 27:51–54, which describes that upon Jesus's death there were earthquakes and that one of the Roman guards stated, "Truly this was the Son of God."[2] He omits entirely the description in Matthew 28 of Jesus's resurrection from the dead and his appearance to his disciples before ascending into Heaven. Instead the Jefferson Bible concludes with the burial of Jesus, the last event of the Gospels that fits with the laws of science.

The Founding Fathers of the United States believed in the importance of religious freedom.

How to Apply Religious Criticism to *The Life and Morals of Jesus of Nazareth*

What Is Religious Criticism?

Religious literary critics analyze the beliefs of a particular religion and consider the current events that shape religious thought and literature. For example, when Jefferson compiled his version of the Bible, he was heavily influenced by the social and intellectual trends of the Enlightenment era.

Applying Religious Criticism to *The Life and Morals of Jesus of Nazareth*

Many early American settlers felt their own particular set of beliefs represented the only correct way to practice their faith, usually Christianity. Individuals who had different beliefs were often ridiculed or persecuted. Jefferson was a follower of deism, a philosophy of faith that declares a belief

Thesis Statement

The thesis of the essay states, "Jefferson's Enlightenment beliefs that religion should be based on reason led him to create his own version of the Christian Bible." The author will assert that the writing of the Jefferson Bible was a direct result of the Enlightenment's influence on Jefferson.

Argument One

This first argument is: "The primary aim of the Age of Enlightenment was the examination of every aspect of life using science and reasoning." It explains the major tenets of the Enlightenment because understanding them is the foundation for the rest of the arguments.

in God based on reason and the natural laws of the universe. In this philosophy, personal experience is combined with a focus on free thinking rather than accepting divine revelations and holy texts. Jefferson's Enlightenment beliefs that religion should be based on reason led him to create his own version of the Christian Bible.

The primary aim of the Age of Enlightenment was the examination of every aspect of life using science and reasoning. Prominent thinkers such as Jefferson held that reason and logic should govern all aspects of life, including government, religion, and other civic factors. Many of the nation's founders were educated and logical individuals who shared this philosophy.

Scientific reasoning and practical thinking had major roles in shaping the future of the United

Thomas Paine, a leading Enlightenment thinker, strongly advocated for an independent America in his pamphlet *Common Sense* (1776).

States of America during the eighteenth century. In his revolutionary document published in 1807, titled *The Age of Reason*, Founding Father, political activist, and author Thomas Paine discussed scientific reason and religion:

> *It is only by the exercise of reason that man can discover God. Take away that reason, and he would be incapable of understanding anything; and, in this case, it would be just as consistent to read even the book called the Bible to a horse as to a man.*[1]

Argument Two

Argument two states, "Jefferson was a strong advocate for religious privacy, freedom of religion and conscience, and the right of an individual to practice any doctrine." This argument shows how the Enlightenment affected Jefferson's political beliefs.

Jefferson was a strong advocate for religious privacy, freedom of religion and conscience, and the right of an individual to practice any doctrine. He believed religion was a private matter between an individual and his God. In fact, even close family members were unaware of Jefferson's particular stance regarding religion and only learned of his modified versions of the Gospels after his death. At a few points in his life, his personal beliefs made him stand out as a subject of ridicule. But his conviction that religion was a private matter prevailed and went a long way in ensuring religious freedom in the future of the United States.

Jefferson's views on religion are set forth in the Virginia Statute for Religious Freedom, which was voted into law in 1786, and in which Jefferson writes:

> *Be it therefore enacted by the General*
> *Assembly, That no man shall be compelled*
> *to frequent or support any religious worship*
> *. . . nor shall be enforced, restrained . . .*

nor shall otherwise suffer on account of his
religious opinions or belief; but that all men
shall be free to profess, and . . . maintain,
their opinions in matters of religion, and
that the same shall in no wise diminish,
enlarge, or affect their civil capacities.[2]

This quote shows Jefferson's commitment to religious freedom and his belief in the fundamental necessity of a separation between church and state. Jefferson does not reject religion; he rejects religion that is forced on people by the government. He asserts that people should be allowed to freely express their religion or lack of religious beliefs without fear of punishment.

Jefferson understood that many believers of different sects reject as false all religious teachings other than their own specific doctrine. However, he showed tolerance toward the beliefs held by others. On December 9, 1805, Jefferson became the first US president to host an interfaith religious dinner. The guest of honor was a Tunisian ambassador, who was a practitioner of Islam. Jefferson and the Tunisian ambassador were to meet during the middle of Ramadan, a dawn-to-dusk fasting ritual performed by followers of Islam. Jefferson held the dinner later in the day to accommodate the ambassador's need to break his ritual fast at sunset.

Jefferson himself rejected religion that was not based on scientific reasoning. Building on his Enlightenment background, Jefferson chose to reexamine religious scriptures from a scientific and rational point of view by creating his own edition of the Bible. Since Jefferson was a strong believer in the philosophical, scientific, and political teachings of Enlightenment thinkers, it was no wonder he applied similar teachings to faith and religion. Jefferson believed Jesus was not a divine being and also questioned the existence of miracles and unexplained phenomena in his life and teachings. Based on correspondence between various friends and family members, it is clear Jefferson believed Jesus was a simple human who had a religious message for the people of the world. According to Jefferson, Jesus and his teachings were wrongly portrayed by religious zealots who believed Jesus himself to be God. Jefferson believed

> **Argument Three**
>
> "Building on his Enlightenment background, Jefferson chose to reexamine religious scriptures from a scientific and rational point of view by creating his own edition of the Bible." The third argument builds on the previous argument and brings the written work of Jefferson into the equation.

Jesus was falsely glorified and his teachings embellished with miracles and mystical phenomena. This was done in the hope Christianity would gain more prominence as a religion and, because it was described as divine revelation, believers would not question its validity. In a letter penned in 1819 to friend William Short, Jefferson wrote:

> *The immaculate conception of Jesus, his deification, the creation of the world by him, his miraculous powers, his resurrection and visible ascension, his corporeal presence in the Eucharist, the Trinity; original sin, atonement, regeneration, election, orders of Hierarchy, etc. [were all] invented by ultra-Christian sects, unauthorized by a single word ever uttered by him.*[3]

The Jefferson Bible is the most concrete evidence of how Enlightenment philosophy affected Jefferson's views of Christianity. In his version of the scripture, he removes the supernatural from the Gospels and focuses on the moral teachings of Jesus. For instance, Jefferson includes almost all of Matthew 5–7, known for its moral teachings, in his version of the Bible. However, he omits Matthew 8, which describes several miracles performed by

Jesus. Jefferson retains the Bible's story of the crucifixion including almost every detail, but ends the story with the burial of Jesus. He skips the supernatural resurrection of Jesus because it does not fit with his reason-based understanding of Christianity.

Conclusion

The final paragraph is the conclusion. It reviews the main points of the essay and restates the thesis. This conclusion also offers a final thought on how Jefferson's viewpoint has become an integral part of the US culture.

Jefferson's views on religion, shaped by Enlightenment thinking, laid the foundation for a country that advocates religious freedom with a separation of church and state. Because Jefferson's own religious views were shaped so distinctly by the Enlightenment, his religious beliefs differed from many of his more devout contemporaries. This difference in his own religion led Jefferson to make religious freedom a cornerstone of his political life. In fact, Jefferson's beliefs with regard to religion set the tone for a tradition still followed nearly 200 years after his death, Jefferson's values of religious freedom, expressed in the founding documents of our nation, remain a cornerstone of US culture.

Thinking Critically about *The Life and Morals of Jesus of Nazareth*

Now it is your turn to assess the critique.

Consider these questions:

1. This essay asserts that Jefferson was a strong proponent of freedom of religion because of his own religious beliefs, which differed from those of the majority of society members of his time. What is another reason freedom of religion could be important to Jefferson?

2. Sometimes it is important to understand the historical context of a document. Could this thesis be supported without understanding the Enlightenment? Why or why not?

3. The conclusion should restate the thesis and the main arguments of the essay. Does this conclusion do that effectively? Why or why not?

Other Approaches

A possible way to apply religious literary criticism to a critique of Jefferson's Bible, *The Life and Morals of Jesus of Nazareth*, is shown in the essay above. Religious literary criticism approaches a document by considering the practices and ideology of a particular faith. Two alternate approaches for applying religious literary criticism to Jefferson's *The Life and Morals of Jesus of Nazareth* are discussed below. The first approach addresses Jefferson's dislike of religious zealousness. The second approach considers early American settlers' intolerance toward the private beliefs and human rights of individuals.

Fanaticism and Zealousness

Jefferson's disapproval of religious fanaticism is another reason behind his modification of the Bible. He described the Book of Revelations as "merely the ravings of a maniac, no more worthy nor capable of explanation than the incoherencies of our own nightly dreams."[4] Such illogical thinking contradicted the Enlightenment's focus on rational thought, and in Jefferson's mind, it was capable of breeding dangerous actions. While Jefferson believed in religious tolerance, he had his own concerns about fanaticism and overzealousness. A possible thesis statement addressing these concerns might be: "As an Enlightenment thinker, Jefferson relied on scientific reasoning and rejected religious fanaticism."

Jefferson: Deist or Infidel?

Many early American settlers were devout Christians who did not readily accept or tolerate individuals who questioned their way of practicing their religion. Due to his religious beliefs, some may have thought Jefferson had the makings of an infidel. A possible thesis statement analyzing these concepts could be: "Jefferson kept his own beliefs private in order to avoid coming into conflict in his personal and political life."

Jefferson, drafter of the Declaration of Independence and third US president, remains one of the most important men in US history.

An Overview of
The Autobiography of Thomas Jefferson

Historical Context

Composed in 1821, *The Autobiography of Thomas Jefferson* is an account of Jefferson's early years, the American Revolution, and Jefferson's subsequent political achievements through his time as an ambassador to France. Jefferson began writing the work at the age of 77. His objective was to "begin to make some memoranda and state some recollections of dates & facts concerning myself, for my own more ready reference & for the information of my family."[1] The book includes a rough draft of the Declaration of Independence along with Jefferson's personal remarks on the Articles of Confederation and the US Constitution. He also describes his time as both a representative and governor of Virginia. The description of his years of service in Paris as minister to France includes his observations of the French Revolution. His recollections end shortly after his return from France, as he was unable to finish the account before his death in 1826.

Looking Backward

Jefferson starts the book by reviewing his family background and history. He extends his gratitude to the mentors who provided guidance in his personal, educational, political, and intellectual endeavors. He mentions his immediate family in passing later in the book. However, Jefferson's narrative focuses mostly on the political, including very few observations about his personal life and family.

The majority of the book revolves around the American Revolution and the foundation of the United States of America. Jefferson includes great detail about his time as a delegate at the Second Continental Congress. Jefferson then describes some of the arguments made in Congress for and against declaring independence from Great Britain before giving his own description of his authorship of the Declaration of Independence. This story differs somewhat from the recollections made by fellow committee member John Adams, but they both agree the committee chose Jefferson to be the primary author of the Declaration of Independence. Jefferson includes a copy of the Declaration of Independence that shows portions Congress deleted. Congress also made additions to Jefferson's draft.

The most insightful portions of the book are when Jefferson describes his personal convictions and recalls attempting to pass laws that would reflect the ideals set forth in the Declaration of Independence. It was essential to create laws that supported "Life, Liberty, and the pursuit of Happiness."[2] Jefferson focused on ridding the new United States of British laws that supported a system based on aristocracy. He focused on abolishing entailment, establishing freedom of religion, and creating equal opportunities in education. Jefferson believed enacting these principles of freedom would kill the "aristocracy of wealth, of more harm and danger, than benefit, to make an opening for the aristocracy of virtue and talent."[3]

Jefferson uses a large portion of the book to discuss his firsthand observations of the French Revolution and his thoughts on the actions of Marie

Antoinette, which played a role in prompting the French to rise up against their monarchy. Jefferson admits the detail and length of his autobiography that are devoted to chronicling the French Revolution are "disproportioned to the general scale of my narrative."[4] It is not surprising the French Revolution is so fascinating to Jefferson; he lived in France during the exciting beginnings of the revolution. Furthermore, Jefferson saw the French Revolution as directly possible because of the American Revolution's success. As a prominent member of the American Revolution, Jefferson took pride in the power it gave to other oppressed peoples to rise up against their corrupt governments. Jefferson's description of the French government relies on terms such as "monstrous abuses," "inequality," "shackles," "cruelty," and "atrocities."[5] He supports the revolutionaries against this "abusive government."[6] However, he admits, "We are but in the first chapter of its history."[7]

Throughout his life, Jefferson aimed to have a positive impact on society. His political career was focused on creating a spirit of independence. This attitude made Jefferson the ideal author of the Declaration of Independence. The words he wrote

Jefferson, memorialized in statue form in Paris, witnessed the first stirrings of the French Revolution while serving as trade commissioner and minister to France.

in that famous document were the principles that he supported the rest of his life. He was devoted to an equal opportunity education system, freedom of religion with a separation between church and state, and choice in passing on property. Jefferson's detailed descriptions of the French Revolution show his excitement that the principles of liberty he had worked to establish in the United States were spreading across the globe. Unfortunately, Jefferson died before completing descriptions of his time as vice president and president, but the descriptions he did leave behind show his overwhelming commitment to liberty.

Jefferson considered Marie Antoinette to be largely responsible for the French Revolution.

How to Apply Feminist Criticism to *The Autobiography of Thomas Jefferson*

What Is Feminist Criticism?

Feminist criticism was born out of the women's movement of the 1960s. The foundation of feminism is a belief that women should have rights, opportunities, and respect equal to men. Feminist critiques often focuses on how a male or female author promotes gender stereotypes of the time period in which the work was written.

One focus of feminist criticism is the lack of women in historical accounts. For instance, most primary and secondary sources covering American history are told from the perspective of white males. Feminist criticism seeks to establish the importance of women in history, despite the prevalent prejudice against women. A feminist critique might focus on one or more of the following questions: Are women mentioned in the work? Were there women who should have been mentioned that were overlooked? When women are mentioned, how are they portrayed?

Applying Feminist Criticism to *The Autobiography of Thomas Jefferson*

The American Revolution was a male-dominated political arena that reflected the beliefs of its time. Women, who had virtually no political say in the war whatsoever, were relegated to the home, considered unfit to make the difficult decisions of politics and government. Thomas Jefferson's autobiography demonstrates this precedent. Although Jefferson fathered five daughters, he hardly mentions them or his wife as he tells the story of his life. The woman to whom Jefferson grants the most words is Queen Marie Antoinette of France, but he only describes her to lay the fault of the French Revolution at her feet. Similar to the political arena of the American Revolution, *The Autobiography of Thomas*

Thesis Statement

The thesis should occur in the last sentence of the first paragraph of a critique. This thesis argues, "Similar to the political arena of the American Revolution, *The Autobiography of Thomas Jefferson* is a male-dominated narrative that reflects the bias of early America that women should have no place in government."

Jefferson is a male-dominated narrative that reflects the bias of early America that women should have no place in government.

Colonial America was a society in which women held power within the home but no power in the government that ruled it. Women were expected to run the family and household while assisting their husbands in the family business of farming or trade. Jefferson's wife, Martha, would have managed the large household while Jefferson traveled for his political career. Despite having power at home, women were not allowed to hold public office, vote, or be a member of the military.

The Founding Fathers held firmly to the male hierarchy despite its inconsistencies with their views on freedom. Thomas Jefferson wrote in the Declaration of Independence that people were given "certain unalienable rights"

Argument One

The author's first argument is, "Colonial America was a society in which women held power within the home but no power in the government that ruled it." The first argument establishes the rights of women within the greater society as the foundation for Jefferson's treatment of women in his autobiography.

Argument Two

The second argument states, "The Founding Fathers held firmly to the male hierarchy despite its inconsistencies with their views on freedom." This establishes the common attitude toward women among the Founding Fathers as the foundation for the arguments to follow.

---

by their Creator, but he did not pass on the same rights and freedoms to women that were given to men.[1] Founding Father John Adams also wanted to maintain male power over women. When his wife Abigail asks John in a letter to "remember the ladies" as he worked at the Continental Congress to establish the new government, Adams finds her request laughable.[2] The idea that women might rise against men in a revolution for equal freedom is quickly dismissed by Adams in his response. These are just two examples of the predominant attitude toward women held by the Founding Fathers who had committed their lives to freedom from oppression.

While describing his life, Thomas Jefferson allows only a few words to mention his wife and daughters. When Jefferson recounts his marriage, he gives it one paragraph, but only one sentence mentions his wife, Martha. The three other sentences in the paragraph are devoted to describing Martha's father and the inheritance he left the couple

Argument Three

The main focus of argument three is how this negative attitude toward women described in the previous arguments explains Jefferson's lack of description of his wife and daughters. It states, "While describing his life, Thomas Jefferson allows only a few words to mention his wife and daughters."

Martha Jefferson Randolph, Jefferson's eldest daughter and his caretaker in his later years, was barely mentioned in Jefferson's autobiography. She inherited Monticello.

upon his death. Jefferson very briefly alludes to the untimely death of his wife in 1782 at the age of 33. The births of his five daughters and one son, of whom only two daughters survived to adulthood, are not even mentioned. The two daughters who did not die in childhood are mentioned only five times in Jefferson's autobiography, each time only because their lives affected his political travels or duties in some way. In only one occurrence does

Jefferson mention one of their names; the other times he just refers to them as daughters.

Jefferson's lack of detail about his wife and daughters shows the lack of importance he placed on them. He chooses to go into extensive detail about the American and French Revolutions, but mentions the death of his wife so briefly he does not use her name. He was not writing a historical account of the revolution, but an autobiography. The very few words committed to his wife and daughters demonstrate how the political focus of the American Revolution on men decreased the importance of his wife and daughters in his eyes.

The only woman Jefferson discusses in detail is Marie Antoinette, but he only gives her attention to blame the French Revolution on her political influence. Jefferson describes King Louis XVI as weak and easily persuaded. He then describes Marie Antoinette as "haughty and bearing no contradiction," and as having

---

Argument Four

The fourth argument says, "The only woman Jefferson discusses in detail is Marie Antoinette, but he only gives her attention to blame the French Revolution on her political influence." This argument shows the contrast between his lack of description of his wife and daughters to the detail he uses to argue that Marie Antoinette's influence over King Louis XVI led to the French Revolution.

"an absolute ascendency over him." Jefferson claims the king would receive good advice in the morning, but it "would be reversed in the evening by the influence of the Queen and court."[3] Later, Jefferson again calls the king "timid" and "weak" and the queen "proud, disdainful of restraint, indignant at all obstacles to her will, eager in the pursuit of pleasure, and firm enough to hold to her desires, or perish in their wreck."[4] These descriptions of King Louis XVI help cast him in a defenseless position without responsibility for the French Revolution. In contrast, Jefferson's descriptions of the queen assert she is a conniving wife seeking pleasure and power at any cost.

Jefferson's most condemning assessment of Marie Antoinette is this bold statement: "I have ever believed that had there been no queen, there would have been no revolution."[5] History shows that Marie Antoinette did play a role in the French Revolution, but Jefferson blames it completely on her. Jefferson's spotlight on Marie Antoinette makes her an example of what may happen if a woman is allowed too much power in government.

The Autobiography of Thomas Jefferson shows Jefferson's male-centered approach to his life

Conclusion

The last paragraph of a critique offers a conclusion. It should restate the thesis and supporting arguments. It also offers a final thought about the paradox of Jefferson's support of freedom and his acceptance of the way colonial America subjugated women.

and politics. Jefferson was a product of his political climate. In colonial America, women were not allowed to take part in government; their focus was supposed to be on their homes and children. The Founding Fathers did not extend to women the freedoms they were fighting against Great Britain to gain, creating an inconsistency in how they applied the principles they fought for. Jefferson's autobiography shows how little importance he placed on women by mentioning his wife and daughters only briefly. The woman he spends time describing is Marie Antoinette, but only to support his notion that the blame for the French Revolution rests on the queen, not King Louis XVI. Jefferson's treatment of women in his autobiography shows his acceptance of a society that did not give women the respect and rights he spent his life protecting.

Thinking Critically about *The Autobiography of Thomas Jefferson*

Now it is your turn to assess the critique. Consider these questions:

1. The first and second arguments are similar. How would you combine them to form one concise argument?

2. Do you agree that a lack of detail about Jefferson's wife and daughters shows he considered them unimportant? What other reason could be given for his lack of coverage of his family in his autobiography?

3. A conclusion should restate the thesis and main arguments. Are there any sentences in the conclusion that could be removed or simplified? Remove or modify one sentence and explain your reasoning.

Other Approaches

Feminist criticism offers a variety of approaches to apply to a chosen work of literature. It focuses on how women are presented as either equals or inferiors to men. Another approach to *The Autobiography of Thomas Jefferson* might consider how Jefferson uses stereotypes about women in his portrayal of Marie Antoinette. A different approach could highlight the women who were important in Jefferson's life that he chose to leave out of his autobiography.

The Overpowering Wife

One common stereotype in literature and other visual arts is a wife who dominates and controls her weak husband behind the scenes. Jefferson's descriptions of Marie Antoinette could be compared with this stereotype to create a feminist critique. A thesis exploring this idea might read, "Jefferson's treatment of Marie Antoinette relies on the stereotype of the domineering wife and her henpecked mate to paint King Louis XVI as a victim."

A Woman Scorned

When Thomas Jefferson was in Paris, he had
a romance with a married British-Italian woman
named Maria Cosway. Although history believes
Maria had a profound impact on Jefferson, he does
not include her in his autobiographical sketch of
his time in Paris. A critique that focused on this
omission could argue, "Jefferson's omission of
Maria Cosway from his autobiography shows that
while Jefferson valued women in his life, he ignored
them in descriptions of politics."

You Critique It

Now that you have learned about different critical theories and how to apply them to different works, are you ready to perform your own critique? You have read that this type of evaluation can help you look at books, speeches, and essays in new ways and make you pay attention to certain issues you may not have otherwise recognized. So, why not use one of the critical theories profiled in this book to consider a fresh take on your favorite work?

First, choose a theory and the work you want to analyze. Remember that the theory is a springboard for asking questions about the work.

Next, write a specific question that relates to the theory you have selected. Then you can form your thesis, which should provide the answer to that question. Your thesis is the most important part of your critique and offers an argument about the work based on the tenets, or beliefs, of the theory you are applying. Recall that the thesis statement typically appears at the very end of the introductory paragraph of your essay. It is usually only one sentence long.

After you have written your thesis, find evidence to back it up. Good places to start are in the work itself or in journals or articles that discuss what other people have said about it. If you are critiquing an essay, you may also want to read about the speaker's life so you can get a sense of what factors may have affected the creation of the essay. This can be especially useful if working within historical or biographical criticism.

Depending on which theory you are applying, you can often find evidence in the work's language, structure, or historical context. You should also explore parts of the work that seem to disprove your thesis and create an argument against them. As you do this, you might want to address what other critics have written about the work. Their quotes may help support your claim.

Before you start analyzing a work, think about the different arguments made in this book. Reflect on how evidence supporting the thesis was presented. Did you find that some of the techniques used to back up the arguments were more convincing than others? Try these methods as you prove your thesis in your own critique.

When you are finished writing your critique, read it over carefully. Is your thesis statement understandable? Do the supporting arguments flow logically, with the topic of each paragraph clearly stated? Can you add any information that would present your readers with a stronger argument in favor of your thesis? Were you able to use quotes from the work, as well as from other critics, to enhance your ideas?

Did you see the work in a new light?

Timeline

1743 Thomas Jefferson is born at Shadwell on April 13.

1757 Jefferson's father, Peter Jefferson, dies on August 17.

1782 After the birth of Lucy Elizabeth, the second of that name, Martha Jefferson takes ill and dies four months later.

1783 Jefferson is elected as a delegate to Congress.

1784 Congress sends Jefferson to France as a trade commissioner and minister; Jefferson's daughter Lucy Elizabeth dies.

1785 *Notes on the State of Virginia* is first printed.

1790 Jefferson takes office as first United States Secretary of State.

1797 Jefferson begins his term as vice president.

1801 Jefferson begins the first of two terms as president.

1803 The Louisiana Purchase is concluded. Lewis and Clark launch their expedition.

1809 After two terms as president, Jefferson retires from public life.

1760 Thomas Jefferson begins attending the College of William and Mary.

1762 Jefferson begins studying law with George Wythe.

1767 Jefferson is admitted to practice law.

1772 Jefferson marries Martha Wayles Skelton on January 1. Later that year, his daughter Martha is born.

1775 Jefferson is elected to the Second Continental Congress.

1776 Jefferson drafts the Declaration of Independence. Afterward, he is elected to the Virginia General Assembly and begins revising Virginia's laws.

1777 Jefferson drafts the Virginia Statute for Religious Freedom.

1779 Jefferson begins serving as governor of Virginia. His term ends in 1781.

1825 The University of Virginia opens its doors

1826 On July 4, Jefferson dies at Monticello.

Glossary

allegiance
Loyalty to a person, group, or cause.

anomalous
Different from what is usual or expected.

aristocratic
Belonging to a high social class.

bile
A bodily fluid.

depreciation
A drop in value or worth.

despotism
A system of government in which the ruler holds all the power.

elite
The best of a group.

Enlightenment
A cultural movement of the seventeenth and eighteenth centuries that relied on rational thought, science and reasoning rather than faith and tradition.

entail
Placing a restriction; limiting land inheritance to direct descendants.

grievance
A cause of distress or complaint.

hierarchy
> The division of a group of people according
> to ability or to economic, social, or
> professional standing.

infidel
> A person who is not Christian or a person who does
> not believe in a religion.

monarchy
> Absolute power or rule by a single person.

patriarchal
> Male-dominated.

sovereign
> Possessing and exercising supreme power.

usurpation
> The act of seizing and using something (such as
> power or land) without having the right to do so.

Bibliography of Works and Criticism

Important Works

"A Summary View of the Rights of British America,"
1774

The Declaration of Independence, 1776

Virginia Statute for Religious Freedom, 1777

Notes on the State of Virginia, 1787

First Inaugural Address, 1801

First Annual Message to Congress, 1801

Second Inaugural Address, 1805

Fifth Annual Message to Congress, 1805

Sixth Annual Message to Congress, 1806

The Autobiography of Thomas Jefferson, 1821

*Jefferson's Bible: The Life and Morals of Jesus of
Nazareth*, 1904

Critical Discussions

Kiernan, Denise. *Signing Their Lives Away: The Fame and Misfortune of the Men Who Signed the Declaration of Independence*. Philadelphia: Quirk, 2009. Print.

Maier, Pauline. *From Resistance to Revolution: Colonial Radicals and the Development of American Opposition to Britain, 1765–1776*. New York: Norton, 1992. Print.

Morgan, Edmund S. *American Slavery, American Freedom: The Ordeal of Colonial Virginia*. New York: Norton, 2003. Print.

Watts, Edward. *Writing and Post-Colonialism in the Early Republic*. Virginia: U of Virginia P, 1998. Print.

Waugh, Patricia. *Literary Theory And Criticism: An Oxford Guide*. New York: Oxford UP, 2006. Print.

Resources

Selected Bibliography

Beran, Michael Knox. *Jefferson's Demons: Portrait of a Restless Mind*. New York: Free Press, 2003. Print.

Hitchens, Christopher. *Thomas Jefferson: Author of America*. New York: Atlas, 2005. Print.

Jefferson, Thomas. *Thomas Jefferson: Thoughts on War and Revolution*. Ed. Brett F. Woods. New York: Algora, 2009. Print.

Jefferson, Thomas. *The Life and Selected Writings of Thomas Jefferson*. Ed. Adrienne Koch and William Peden. New York: Random, 1993. Print.

Further Readings

Mullin, Rita Thievon. *Thomas Jefferson: Architect of Freedom*. New York: Sterling, 2007. Print.

Zinn, Howard. *A People's History of the United States*. New York: Harper, 2003. Print.

Web Links

To learn more about critiquing the works of
Thomas Jefferson, visit ABDO Publishing Company
online at **www.abdopublishing.com**. Web sites
about the works of Thomas Jefferson are featured
on our Book Links page. These links are routinely
monitored and updated to provide the most current
information available.

For More Information

Monticello
Post Office Box 316, Charlottesville, VA 22902
434-984-9800
www.monticello.org

Located near Charlottesville, Virginia, Monticello is the
only historic house in the United States on the list of
UNESCO World Heritage Sites.

Thomas Jefferson Memorial
National Mall and Memorial Parks
900 Ohio Drive SW, Washington DC 20024
202-426-6841
www.nps.gov/thje/index.htm

Opened in 1934, the Thomas Jefferson Memorial
celebrates the third president of the United States. It is
located on the National Mall near the Lincoln Memorial.

Source Notes

Chapter 1. Introduction to Critiques

None.

Chapter 2. A Closer Look at Thomas Jefferson

1. "Jefferson's Gravestone." *Jefferson Monticello.*
Thomas Jefferson Foundation, 1996–2012. Web.
18 Sept. 2012.

**Chapter 3. An Overview of the Declaration
of Independence**

1. George M. Stephens. *Locke, Jefferson, and
the Justices: Foundations and Failures of the US
Government.* New York: Algora, 2002. Print. 50.

2. "Declaration of Independence." *Digital
Collections: Rare Book and Special Collections
Division.* Library of Congress, n.d. Web. 18 Sept. 2012.

3. Ibid.

4. Ibid.

5. Ibid.

6. Ibid.

7. Ibid.

**Chapter 4. How to Apply Historical Criticism to the
Declaration of Independence**

1. "Declaration of Independence." *Digital
Collections: Rare Book and Special Collections
Division.* Library of Congress, n.d. Web. 18 Sept. 2012.

2. Ibid.

3. Ibid.

4. Ibid.

Chapter 5. An Overview of *Notes on the State of Virginia*

1. Thomas Jefferson. *Notes on the State of Virginia*. Boston, 1832. *Google Book Search*. Web. 31 Oct. 2012.

2. Ibid.

3. Ibid.

4. Ibid.

Chapter 6. How to Apply Biographical Criticism to *Notes on the State of Virginia*

1. Howard Zinn. *A People's History of the United States*. New York: Harper, 2003. Print. 31.

2. Thomas Jefferson. *Notes on the State of Virginia*. Boston, 1832. *Google Book Search*. Web. 31 Oct. 2012.

3. Ibid.

4. Ibid.

5. "Entail." *Merriam-Webster*. 2012. Web.

6. Thomas Jefferson. *Notes on the State of Virginia*. Boston, 1832. *Google Book Search*. Web. 31 Oct. 2012.

7. Ibid.

8. "Declaration of Independence." *Digital Collections: Rare Book and Special Collections Division*. Library of Congress, n.d. Web. 18 Sept. 2012.

9. Thomas Jefferson. *Notes on the State of Virginia*. Boston, 1832. *Google Book Search*. Web. 31 Oct. 2012.

Source Notes Continued

10. Ibid.

11. Ibid.

Chapter 7. An Overview of *The Life and Morals of Jesus of Nazareth*

1. Thomas Jefferson. "The Code Of Jesus to John Adams Monticello, Oct. 12, 1813." *Electronic Text Center*. University of Virginia, n.d. Web. 25 May 2012.

2. *The Holy Bible: King James Version*. Peabody, MA: Hendrickson, 2011. Print. 474.

Chapter 8. How to Apply Religious Criticism to *The Life and Morals of Jesus of Nazareth*

1. Thomas Paine. *Writings of Thomas Paine— Volume 4 (1794–1796): The Age of Reason by Thomas Paine*. Ed. Moncure Daniel Conway, 2003. *Project Gutenberg*. Web. 30 May 2012.

2. "The Virginia Act for Establishing Religious Freedom, Thomas Jefferson 1786." *Religious Freedom Page*. Religious Freedom Page, n.d. Web. 31 May 2012.

3. "To William Short." *The Works of Thomas Jefferson*. Federal Edition. New York and London: Putnam, 1904–1905. Vol. 12. *Online Library of Liberty*. Web. 31 Oct. 2012.

4. Charles B. Sandford. *The Religious Life of Thomas Jefferson*. Virginia: U of Virginia, 1984. Print. 122.

Chapter 9. An Overview of *The Autobiography of Thomas Jefferson*

1. Thomas Jefferson. *The Autobiography of Thomas Jefferson*. n.p.: DigiReads.com, 2009. Web. 3.

2. "Declaration of Independence." *Digital Collections: Rare Book and Special Collections Division*. Library of Congress, n.d. Web. 18 Sept. 2012.

3. Thomas Jefferson. *The Autobiography of Thomas Jefferson*. n.p.: DigiReads.com, 2009. Web. 58.

4. Ibid. 155–156.

5. Ibid. 128.

6. Ibid. 105.

7. Ibid. 156.

Chapter 10. How to Apply Feminist Criticism to *The Autobiography of Thomas Jefferson*

1. "Declaration of Independence." Digital Collections: Rare Book and Special Collections Division. *Library of Congress*, n.d. Web. 18 Sept. 2012.

2. "Letter from Abigail Adams to John Adams, 31 March–5 April 1776." *Adams Family Papers: An Electronic Archive*. Massachusetts Historical Society, n.d. Web. 19 Sept. 2012.

3. Thomas Jefferson. *The Autobiography of Thomas Jefferson*. n.p.: DigiReads.com, 2009. Web. 131.

4. Ibid. 149.

5. Ibid.

Index

About the Author

Annie Qaiser is a freelance writer based in Saint Paul, Minnesota. She lives with her husband and family.

Photo Credits

AP Images, cover, 3; Library of Congress, 12, 21, 35, 42, 69, 98; Victorian Traditions/Shutterstock Images, 22; Susan Law Cain/Shutterstock Images, 25; North Wind/North Wind Picture Archives, 30, 47, 50, 66, 89; Tom Williams/Getty Images, 62; Bettman/Corbis/AP Images, 78, 99; Shutterstock Images, 83, 84